Kicking the Leaves

Also by Donald Hall

Kicking the Leaves

poems by

Donald Hall

Harper & Row, Publishers
New York · Hagerstown · San Francisco · London

Grateful acknowledgment is made for permission to reprint some of the poems that appeared in *The American Poetry Review, Green House, Grove, Harvard Magazine, The Iowa Review, The New York Times, Ohio Review,* and *The Virginia Quarterly Review.*

"Photographs of China" originally appeared in *The American Review.*

"Flies" originally appeared in the *Country Journal.* Reprinted by permission of the Country Journal Publishing Company, Brattleboro, Vermont.

"Ox Cart Man" and "Names of Horses" © 1977 The New Yorker Magazine, Inc.

FIRST EDITION

Designed by Gloria Adelson

70972

Library of Congress Cataloging in Publication Data

Hall, Donald, 1928–
    Kicking the leaves.

    I. Title.
PS3515.A3152K52   811'.5'4   78–2055
ISBN 0–06–011704–4   78 79 80 81 82 10 9 8 7 6 5 4 3 2 1
ISBN 0–06–090647–2 pbk. 78 79 80 81 82 10 9 8 7 6 5 4 3 2 1

for Jane Kenyon

Contents

Kicking the Leaves

Eating the Pig

Twelve people, most of us strangers, stand in a room
in Ann Arbor, drinking Cribari from jars.
Then two young men, who cooked him,
carry him to the table
on a large square of plywood: his body
striped, like a tiger cat's, from the basting,
his legs long, much longer than a cat's,
and the striped hide as shiny as vinyl.

Now I see his head, as he takes his place
at the center of the table,
his wide pig's head; and he looks like the *javelina*
that ran in front of the car, in the desert outside Tucson,
and I am drawn to him, my brother the pig,
with his large ears cocked forward,
with his tight snout, with his small ferocious teeth
in a jaw propped open
by an apple. How bizarre, this raw apple clenched
in a cooked face! Then I see his eyes,
his eyes cramped shut, his no-eyes, his eyes like X's
in a comic strip, when the character gets knocked out.

This afternoon they read directions
from a book: *The eyeballs must be removed*
or they will burst during roasting. So they hacked them out.
"I nearly fainted," says someone.
"I never fainted before, in my whole life."
Then they gutted the pig and stuffed him,

and roasted him five hours, basting the long body.

*   *   *

Now we examine him, exclaiming, and we marvel at him—
but no one picks up a knife.

Then a young woman cuts off his head.
It comes off so easily, like a detachable part.
With sudden enthusiasm we dismantle the pig,
we wrench his trotters off, we twist them
at shoulder and hip, and they come off so easily.
Then we cut open his belly and pull the skin back.

For myself, I scoop a portion of left thigh,
moist, tender, falling apart, fat, sweet.

We forage like an army starving in winter
that crosses a pass in the hills and discovers
a valley of full barns—
cattle fat and lowing in their stalls,
bins of potatoes in root cellars under white farmhouses,
barrels of cider, onions, hens squawking over eggs—
and the people nowhere, with bread still warm in the oven.

Maybe, south of the valley, refugees pull their carts
listening for Stukas or elephants, carrying
bedding, pans, and silk dresses,
old men and women, children, deserters, young wives.

12

No, we are here, eating the pig together.

*   *   *

In ten minutes, the destruction is total.

His tiny ribs, delicate as birds' feet, lie crisscrossed.
Or they are like cross-hatching in a drawing,
lines doubling and redoubling on each other.

Bits of fat and muscle
mix with stuffing alien to the body,
walnuts and plums. His skin, like a parchment bag
soaked in oil, is pulled back and flattened,
with ridges and humps remaining, like a contour map,
like the map of a defeated country.

The army consumes every blade of grass in the valley,
every tree, every stream, every village,
every crossroad, every shack, every book, every graveyard.

His intact head
swivels around, to view the landscape of body
as if in dismay.

"For sixteen weeks I lived. For sixteen weeks
I took into myself nothing but the milk of my mother
who rolled on her side for me,

13

for my brothers and sisters. Only five hours roasting,
and this body so quickly dwindles away to nothing.''

*   *   *

By itself, isolated on this plywood,
among this puzzle of foregone possibilities,
his intact head seems to want affection.
Without knowing that I will do it,
I reach out and scratch his jaw,
and I stroke him behind his ears,
as if he might suddenly purr from his cooked head.

"When I stroke your pig's ears,
and scratch the striped leather of your jowls,
the furrow between the sockets of your eyes,
I take into myself, and digest,
wheat that grew between
the Tigris and the Euphrates rivers.

"And I take into myself the flint carving tool,
and the savannah, and hairs in the tail
of Eohippus, and fingers of bamboo,
and Hannibal's elephant, and Hannibal,
and everything that lived before us, everything born,
exalted, and dead, and historians
who carved in the Old Kingdom
when the wall had not heard about China.''

I speak these words
into the ear of the stone-age pig, the Abraham
pig, the ocean pig, the Achilles pig,
and into the ears
of the fire pig that will eat our bodies up.

"Fire, brother and father,
twelve of us, in our different skins, older and younger,
opened your skin together
and tore your body apart, and took it
into our bodies."

O Cheese

In the pantry the dear dense cheeses, Cheddars and harsh
Lancashires; Gorgonzola with its magnanimous manner;
the clipped speech of Roquefort; and a head of Stilton
that speaks in a sensuous riddling tongue like Druids.

O cheeses of gravity, cheeses of wistfulness, cheeses
that weep continually because they know they will die.
O cheeses of victory, cheeses wise in defeat, cheeses
fat as a cushion, lolling in bed until noon.

Liederkranz ebullient, jumping like a small dog, noisy;
Pont l'Evêque intellectual, and quite well informed; Emmentaler
decent and loyal, a little deaf in the right ear;
and Brie the revealing experience, instantaneous and profound.

O cheeses that dance in the moonlight, cheeses
that mingle with sausages, cheeses of Stonehenge.
O cheeses that are shy, that linger in the doorway,
eyes looking down, cheeses spectacular as fireworks.

Reblochon openly sexual; Caerphilly like pine trees, small
at the timberline; Port du Salut in love; Caprice des Dieux
eloquent, tactful, like a thousand-year-old hostess;
and Dolcelatte, always generous to a fault.

O village of cheeses, I make you this poem of cheeses,
O family of cheeses, living together in pantries,
O cheeses that keep to your own nature, like a lucky couple,
this solitude, this energy, these bodies slowly dying.

Wolf Knife

from *The Journals of*
C. F. Hoyt, USN, 1826–1889

"In mid-August, in the second year
of my First Polar Expedition, the snows and ice of winter
almost upon us, Kantiuk and I
attempted to dash by sledge
along Crispin Bay, searching again for relics
of the Franklin Expedition. Now a storm blew,
and we turned back, and we struggled slowly
in snow, lest we depart land and venture onto ice
from which a sudden fog and thaw
would abandon us to the Providence
of the sea.

                              "Near nightfall
I thought I heard snarling behind us.
Kantiuk told me
that two wolves, lean as the bones
of a wrecked ship,
had followed us the last hour, and snapped their teeth
as if already feasting.
I carried but the one charge
in my rifle, since, approaching the second winter,
we rationed stores.

                              "As it turned dark,
we could push no further, and made
camp in a corner
of ice-hummocks,

18

and the wolves stopped also, growling
just past the limits of vision,
coming closer, until I could hear
the click of their feet on ice. Kantiuk laughed
and remarked that the wolves appeared to be most hungry.
I raised my rifle, prepared to shoot the first
that ventured close, hoping
to frighten the other.

"Kantiuk struck my rifle
down, and said again
that the wolves were hungry, and laughed.
I feared that my old companion
was mad, here in the storm, among ice-hummocks,
stalked by wolves. Now Kantiuk searched
in his pack, and extricated
two knives—*turnoks,* the Innuits called them—
which by great labor were sharpened, on both sides,
to a sharpness like the edge of a barber's razor,
and approached our dogs
and plunged both knives
into the body of our youngest dog
who had limped all day.

"I remember
that I considered turning my rifle on Kantiuk
as he approached, then passed me,

carrying knives red with the gore of our dog—
who had yowled, moaned, and now lay
expiring, surrounded
by curious cousins and uncles,
possibly hungry—and thrust the knives
handle-down in the snow.

                              "Immediately
he left the knives, the vague, gray
shapes of the wolves
turned solid, out of the darkness and the snow,
and set ravenously
to licking blood from the honed steel.
The double edge of the knives
so lacerated the tongues of the starved beasts
that their own blood poured
copiously forth
to replenish the dog's blood, and they ate
more furiously than before, while Kantiuk laughed,
and held his sides
laughing.

            "And I laughed also,
perhaps in relief that Providence had delivered us
yet again, or perhaps—under conditions of extremity,
far from Connecticut—finding these creatures
acutely ridiculous, so avid

to swallow their own blood. First one, and then the other
collapsed, dying,
bloodless in the snow black with their own blood,
and Kantiuk retrieved
his *turnoks,* and hacked lean meat
from the thigh of the larger wolf,
which we ate
gratefully, blessing the Creator, for we were hungry."

Photographs of China

After the many courses, hot bowls of rice,
plates of pork, cabbage, duck, and peapods,
we return to Chia-Shun's living room,
to the fire and conversation.
                                        Chia-Shun brings over
an old book of photographs, printed in France.
"I want to show you China," he says,
"our China. This river"—he spreads a page flat—
"my university was beside this river."
The river looks wide, in the sepia photograph,
maybe half a mile wide, geese floating on it, and junks.
Beyond the river, there are rolling darkening hills,
like elephant skin, like the brows of Indian elephants.

"During the war, we bathed ourselves in that river.
Oh, it was cold in the winter!"

                        *   *   *

Li Chi crosses the room, touching the furniture.
She sits on the sofa between us, and peers
into the pages of photographs, her glasses
nearly bumping the pages she turns.
"Here," she says, "is West Lake, which is my home.
I always lived near the water, until now,
in Ann Arbor." Her laugh makes a noise like paper.

"When I was first at the university, in China,
I lived so close to the water

that I could fish out my window!"
                              Later,
we will persuade her to sing a poem from T'ang
that she learned from her mother, in her mother's accents.

                         *   *   *

We sit on the sofa, turning the pages together,
When we come to the river again, the book lies flat,
and Chia-Shun says,
                         "On Sundays,
I would ask my friend to help me prepare my assignment.
Then I spent all day
walking alone in the mountains."
                              There were orange trees
beside the hot springs, even in frosty winter.

"How the gold shone in the green shadows then!"

                         *   *   *

"When I was teaching," Li Chi says, "in another city,
the planes bombed the house where I lived.
Fortunately, I was not home at the time"—she laughs—
"but my clothes, *all* of my clothes,
were up in a tree."
                         Chia-Shun laughs also,
and closes the book, and says,
"When I see these pictures, when I remember these things,"
—he looks like a boy, wild and pink with excitement—
"I want to live two hundred years!"

And Li Chi:
"When I close my eyes, because my eyes hurt me,
then it is West Lake that I see."

Maple Syrup

August, goldenrod blowing. We walk
into the graveyard, to find
my grandfather's grave. Ten years ago
I came here last, bringing
marigolds from the round garden
outside the kitchen.
I didn't know you then.
                      We walk
among carved names that go with photographs
on top of the piano at the farm:
Keneston, Wells, Fowler, Batchelder, Buck.
We pause at the new grave
of Grace Fenton, my grandfather's
sister. Last summer
we called on her at the nursing home,
eighty-seven, and nodding
in a blue housedress. We cannot find
my grandfather's grave.
                    Back at the house
where no one lives, we potter
and explore the back chamber
where everything comes to rest: spinning wheels,
pretty boxes, quilts,
bottles, books, albums of postcards.
Then with a flashlight we descend
firm steps to the root cellar—black,
cobwebby, huge,
with dirt floors and fieldstone walls,

25

and above the walls, holding the hewn
sills of the house, enormous
granite foundation stones.
Past the empty bins
for squash, apples, carrots, and potatoes,
we discover the shelves for canning, a few
pale pints
of tomato left, and—what
is this?—syrup, maple syrup
in a quart jar, syrup
my grandfather made twenty-five
years ago
for the last time.
                 I remember
coming to the farm in March
in sugaring time, as a small boy.
He carried the pails of sap, sixteen-quart
buckets, dangling from each end
of a wooden yoke
that lay across his shoulders, and emptied them
into a vat in the saphouse
where fire burned day and night
for a week.
              Now the saphouse
tilts, nearly to the ground,
like someone exhausted
to the point of death, and next winter
when snow piles three feet thick

on the roofs of the cold farm,
the saphouse will shudder and slide
with the snow to the ground.
                              Today
we take my grandfather's last
quart of syrup
upstairs, holding it gingerly,
and we wash off twenty-five years
of dirt, and we pull
and pry the lid up, cutting the stiff,
dried rubber gasket, and dip our fingers
in, you and I both, and taste
the sweetness, you for the first time,
the sweetness preserved, of a dead man
in his own kitchen,
giving us
from his lost grave the gift of sweetness.

Kicking the Leaves

1.

Kicking the leaves, October, as we walk home together
from the game, in Ann Arbor,
on a day the color of soot, rain in the air;
I kick at the leaves of maples,
reds of seventy different shades, yellow
like old paper; and poplar leaves, fragile and pale;
and elm leaves, flags of a doomed race.
I kick at the leaves, making a sound I remember
as the leaves swirl upward from my boot,
and flutter; and I remember
Octobers walking to school in Connecticut,
wearing corduroy knickers that swished
with a sound like leaves; and a Sunday buying
a cup of cider at a roadside stand
on a dirt road in New Hampshire; and kicking the leaves,
autumn 1955 in Massachusetts, knowing
my father would die when the leaves were gone.

2.

Each fall in New Hampshire, on the farm
where my mother grew up, a girl in the country,
my grandfather and grandmother
finished the autumn work, taking the last vegetables in
from the cold fields, canning, storing roots and apples
in the cellar under the kitchen. Then my grandfather
raked leaves against the house
as the final chore of autumn.
One November I drove up from college to see them.
We pulled big rakes, as we did when we hayed in summer,
pulling the leaves against the granite foundations
around the house, on every side of the house,
and then, to keep them in place, we cut spruce boughs
and laid them across the leaves,
green on red, until the house
was tucked up, ready for snow
that would freeze the leaves in tight, like a stiff skirt.
Then we puffed through the shed door,
taking off boots and overcoats, slapping our hands,
and sat in the kitchen, rocking, and drank
black coffee my grandmother made,
three of us sitting together, silent, in gray November.

3.

One Saturday when I was little, before the war,
my father came home at noon from his half day at the office
and wore his Bates sweater, black on red,
with the crossed hockey sticks on it, and raked beside me
in the back yard, and tumbled in the leaves with me,
laughing, and carried me, laughing, my hair full of leaves,
to the kitchen window
where my mother could see us, and smile, and motion
to set me down, afraid I would fall and be hurt.

4.

Kicking the leaves today, as we walk home together
from the game, among crowds of people
with their bright pennants, as many and bright as leaves,
my daughter's hair is the red-yellow color
of birch leaves, and she is tall like a birch,
growing up, fifteen, growing older; and my son
flamboyant as maple, twenty,
visits from college, and walks ahead of us, his step
springing, impatient to travel
the woods of the earth. Now I watch them
from a pile of leaves beside this clapboard house
in Ann Arbor, across from the school
where they learned to read,
as their shapes grow small with distance, waving,
and I know that I
diminish, not them, as I go first
into the leaves, taking
the step they will follow, Octobers and years from now.

5.

This year the poems came back, when the leaves fell.
Kicking the leaves, I heard the leaves tell stories,
remembering, and therefore looking ahead, and building
the house of dying. I looked up into the maples
and found them, the vowels of bright desire.
I thought they had gone forever
while the bird sang *I love you, I love you*
and shook its black head
from side to side, and its red eye with no lid,
through years of winter, cold
as the taste of chicken wire, the music of cinder block.

6.

Kicking the leaves, I uncover the lids of graves.
My grandfather died at seventy-seven, in March
when the sap was running; and I remember my father
twenty years ago,
coughing himself to death at fifty-two in the house
in the suburbs. Oh, how we flung
leaves in the air! How they tumbled and fluttered around us,
like slowly cascading water, when we walked together
in Hamden, before the war, when Johnson's Pond
had not surrendered to houses, the two of us
hand in hand, and in the wet air the smell of leaves
burning;
and in six years I will be fifty-two.

7.

Now I fall, now I leap and fall
to feel the leaves crush under my body, to feel my body
buoyant in the ocean of leaves, the night of them,
night heaving with death and leaves, rocking like the ocean.
Oh, this delicious falling into the arms of leaves,
into the soft laps of leaves!
Face down, I swim into the leaves, feathery,
breathing the acrid odor of maple, swooping
in long glides to the bottom of October—
where the farm lies curled against winter, and soup steams
its breath of onion and carrot
onto damp curtains and windows; and past the windows
I see the tall bare maple trunks and branches, the oak
with its few brown weathery remnant leaves,
and the spruce trees, holding their green.
Now I leap and fall, exultant, recovering
from death, on account of death, in accord with the dead,
the smell and taste of leaves again,
and the pleasure, the only long pleasure, of taking a place
in the story of leaves.

Traffic

Trucks and stationwagons, VWs, old Chevies, Pintos
drive stop-and-go down Whitney Avenue this hot
May day, bluing the coarse air, past graveyard and florist,
past this empty brick building covered
with ivy like a Mayan temple,
like a pyramid grown over with jungle vines.

                                         I walk around
the building as if I were dreaming it; as if
I had left my planet at twenty
and wandered a lifetime among galaxies and come home
to find my planet aged ten-thousand years,
ruined, grown over,
the people gone, ruin taking their places. . . .

                                         They
have gone into graveyards, who worked at this loading dock
wearing brown uniforms with the pink-and-blue lettering
of the Brock-Hall Dairy:
Freddie Bauer is dead, who watched over the stockroom;
Agnes McSparren is dead, who wrote figures in books
at a yellow wooden desk; Harry Bailey is dead,
who tested for bacteria
wearing a white coat; Karl Kapp is dead
who loaded his van at dawn,
conveyorbelt supplying butter, cottage cheese, heavy cream,
B, buttermilk, A with its creamline—
and left white bottles at backdoors in North Haven and Hamden
for thirty years; my father is dead
and my grandfather.

I stand by the fence at lot's end
where the long stable stood—
fifty workhorses alive
in the suburbs, chestnuts with thick manes, their hooves
the size of oak stumps, that pulled forty thousand quarts
through mists in the early morning to sleeping doorsteps,
until new trucks jammed the assembly lines
when the war ended. . . .
                I separate ivy
like long hair over a face
to gaze into the room where the bottlewasher
stretched its aluminum length like an Airstream trailer.
When our teacher brought the first grade to the dairy,
men in white caps stacked dirty bottles
at the machine's end, and we heard them clink
forty feet to where they rode out shining
on a belt to another machine
that turned them instantly white, as if someone said a word
that turned them white. I was proud
of my father and grandfather,
of my last name.
                Here is the place
that was lettered with my father's name,
where he parked his Oldsmobile in the fifties.
I came to the plant with him one summer
when I was at college, and we walked across blacktop
where people my age washed trucks;
both of us smiled and looked downwards. That year

the business grossed sixteen million dollars
with four hundred people bottling and delivering milk
and Agnes McSparren was boss
over thirty women.
                                    At the roof's edge,
imperial Roman cement urns
flourish and decorate exhausted air.
Now suburbs have migrated north
leaving Whitneyville behind, with its dead factory
beside a dead movie. They lived in Whitneyville
mostly—Freddie Bauer, Agnes McSparren, Karl Kapp,
Harry Bailey—who walked their lives
into brick, whose hours turned into milk,
who left their lives inside pitted brick
that disappears beneath ivy
for a thousand years, until the archeologist from a far galaxy
chops with his machete. . . .
                                    No, no, no . . .
In a week or a year
the wrecker's derrick with fifteen-ton cement ball
on a flatbed trailer
will stop traffic as it squeezes up Whitney Avenue,
and brick will collapse, and dump trucks take clean fill
for construction rising from a meadow
ten miles in the country.
                                    I wait
for the traffic to pause, shift, and enter the traffic.

Flies

for Kate Wells 1878–1975

A fly sleeps on the field of a green curtain. I sit by my grand-mother's side, and rub her head as if I could comfort her. Ninety-seven years. Her eyes stay closed, her mouth open, and she gasps in her blue nightgown—pale blue, washed a thousand times. Now her face goes white, and her breath slows until I think it has stopped; then she gasps again, and pink returns to her face.

Between the roof of her mouth and her tongue, strands of spittle waver as she breathes. Now a nurse shakes her head over my grandmother's sore mouth, and goes to get a glass of water, a spoon, and a flyswatter. My grandmother chokes on a spoonful of water and the nurse swats the fly.

* * *

In the Connecticut suburbs where I grew up, and in Ann Arbor, there were houses with small leaded panes, where Formica shone in the kitchens, and hardwood in closets under paired leather boots. Carpets lay thick underfoot in every bedroom, bright, clean, with no dust or hair in them. Nothing looked used, in these houses. Forty dollars worth of cut flowers leaned from Waterford vases for the Saturday dinner party.

Even in houses like these, the housefly wandered and paused—and I listened for the buzz of its wings and its tiny feet, as it struggled among cut flowers and bumped into leaded panes.

* * *

In the afternoon my mother takes over at my grandmother's side in the Peabody Home, while I go back to the farm. I nap in the room my mother and my grandmother were born in.

At night we assemble beside her. Her shallow, rapid breath rasps, and her eyes jerk, and the nurse can find no pulse, as her small strength concentrates wholly on half an inch of lung space, and she coughs faintly—quick coughs like fingertips on a ledge. Her daughters stand by the bed, solemn in the slow evening, in the shallows of after-supper—Caroline, Nan, and Lucy, her eldest daughter, seventy-two, who holds her hand to help her die, as twenty years past she did the same thing for my father.

Then her breath slows again, as it has done all day. Pink vanishes from cheeks we have kissed so often, and her nostrils quiver. She breathes one more quick breath. Her mouth twitches sharply, as if she speaks a word we cannot hear. Her face is fixed, white, her eyes half-closed, and the next breath never comes.

*　　*　　*

She lies in a casket covered with gray linen, which my mother and her sisters picked. This is Chadwick's Funeral Parlor in New London, on the ground floor under the I.O.O.F. Her fine hair lies combed on the pillow. Her teeth in, her mouth closed, she looks the way she used to, except that her face is tinted, tanned as if she worked in the fields.

This air is so still it has bars. Because I have been thinking about flies, I realize that there are no flies in this room. I imagine a fly wandering in, through these dark-curtained windows, to land on my grandmother's nose.

At the Andover graveyard, Astroturf covers the dirt beside the shaft dug for her. Mr. Jones says a prayer beside the open hole. He preached at the South Danbury Church when my grandmother still played the organ. He raises his narrow voice, that gives itself over to August and blue air, and tells us that Kate in heaven "will keep on growing . . . and growing . . . and growing . . ."—and he stops abruptly, as if the sky had abandoned him, and chose to speak elsewhere through someone else.

* * *

After the burial I walk by myself in the barn where I spent summers next to my grandfather. I think of them talking in heaven. Her first word is the word her mouth was making when she died.

In this tie-up a chaff of flies roiled in the leather air, as my grandfather milked his Holsteins morning and night, his bald head pressed sweating into their sides, fat female Harlequins, while their black and white tails swept back and forth, stirring the flies up. His voice spoke pieces he learned for the Lyceum, and I listened crouched on a three-legged stool, as his hands kept time *strp strp* with alternate streams of hot milk, the sound softer as milk foamed to the pail's top.

In the tie-up the spiders feasted like emperors. Each April he broomed the webs out and whitewashed the wood, but spiders and flies came back, generation on generation—like the cattle, mothers and daughters, for a hundred and fifty years, until my grandfather's heart flapped in his chest. One by one the slow Holsteins climbed the ramp into a cattle truck.

* * *

In the kitchen with its bare hardwood floor, my grandmother stood by the clock's mirror to braid her hair every morning. She looked out the window towards Kearsarge, and said, "Mountain's pretty today," or, "Can't see the mountain too good today."

She fought the flies all summer. She shut the screen door *quickly,* but flies gathered on cannisters, on the clockface, on the range when the fire was out, on set-tubs, tables, curtains, chairs. Flies buzzed on cooling lard, when my grandmother made doughnuts. Flies lit on a drip of jam before she could wipe it up. Flies whirled over simmering beans, in the steam of maple syrup.

My grandmother fretted, and took good aim with a flyswatter, and hung strips of flypaper behind the range where nobody would tangle her hair in it.

She gave me a penny for every ten I killed. All day with my mesh flyswatter I patrolled kitchen and diningroom, livingroom, even the dead air of the parlor. Though I killed every fly in the house by bedtime, when my grandmother washed the hardwood floor, by morning their sons and cousins assembled in the kitchen, like the woodchucks my grandfather shot in the vegetable garden, that doubled and returned; or like the deer that watched for a hundred and fifty years from the brush on Ragged Mountain, and when my grandfather died stalked down the mountainside to graze among peas and corn.

*   *   *

We live in their house with our books and pictures, writing poems under Ragged Mountain, gazing each morning at blue Kearsarge.

I dream one night that we live here together, four of us, Jane and I with Kate and Wesley. He milks the cows, she tends sheep and chickens. When we wake one morning the two old people are gone, and their animals gone also. In my dream I know they are dead. All

morning we look for their bodies in tall grass around barn and
chickencoop, until at noon we look up and see them walking the
dirt road from West Andover, waving their arms to catch our
attention, laughing with pleasure at our surprise, leading a column
of giraffes and zebras, ostriches, lions, parrots, gorillas, and tigers
up to the house and to the barn.

*   *   *

We live in the house left behind; we sleep in the bed where they
whispered together at night. One morning I wake hearing a voice
from sleep: "The blow of the axe resides in the acorn."

I get out of bed and drink cold water in the dark morning from
the sink's dipper at the window under the sparse oak, and a fly
wakes buzzing beside me, cold, and sweeps over set-tubs and range,
one of the hundred-thousandth generation.

I planned long ago I would live here, somebody's grandfather.

The Black Faced Sheep

Ruminant pillows! Gregarious soft boulders!

If one of you found a gap in a stone wall,
the rest of you—rams, ewes, bucks, wethers, lambs;
mothers and daughters, old grandfather-father,
cousins and aunts, small bleating sons—
followed onward, stupid
as sheep, wherever
your leader's sheep-brain wandered to.

My grandfather spent all day searching the valley
and edges of Ragged Mountain,
calling "Ke-*day!*" as if he brought you salt,
"Ke-*day! Ke-day!*"

           *   *   *

When a bobcat gutted a lamb at the Keneston place
in the spring of eighteen-thirteen
a hundred and fifty frightened black faced sheep
lay in a stupor and died.

           *   *   *

When the shirt wore out, and darns in the woolen
shirt needed darning,
a woman in a white collar
cut the shirt into strips and braided it,
as she braided her hair every morning.

In a hundred years
the knees of her great-granddaughter
crawled on a rug made from the wool of sheep
whose bones were mud,
like the bones of the woman, who stares
from an oval in the parlor.

                    *   *   *

I forked the brambly hay down to you
in nineteen-fifty. I delved my hands deep
in the winter grass of your hair.

When the shearer cut to your nakedness in April
and you dropped black eyes in shame,
hiding in barnyard corners, unable to hide,
I brought grain to raise your spirits,
and ten thousand years
wound us through pasture and hayfield together,
threads of us woven
together, three hundred generations
from Africa's hills to New Hampshire's.

                    *   *   *

You were not shrewd like the pig.
You were not strong like the horse.
You were not brave like the rooster.

Yet none of the others looked like a lump of granite
that grew hair,
and none of the others
carried white fleece as soft as dandelion seed
around a black face,
and none of them sang such a flat and sociable song.

*   *   *

In November a bearded man, wearing a lambskin apron,
slaughtered an old sheep for mutton
and hung the carcass in north shade
and cut from the frozen sides all winter, to stew in a pot
on the fire that never went out.

*   *   *

Now the black faced sheep have wandered and will not return,
though I search the valleys
and call "Ke-*day*" as if I brought them salt.

Now the railroad draws
a line of rust through the valley. Birch, pine, and maple
lean from cellarholes
and cover the dead pastures of Ragged Mountain
except where machines make snow
and cables pull money up hill, to slide back down.

*   *   *

At South Danbury Church twelve of us sit—
cousins and aunts, sons—

45

where the great-grandfathers of the forty-acre farms
filled every pew.
I look out the window at summer places,
at Boston lawyers' houses
with swimming pools cunningly added to cowsheds,
and we read an old poem aloud, about Israel's sheep
—and I remember faces and wandering hearts,
dear lumps of wool—and we read

that the rich farmer, though he names his farm for himself,
takes nothing into his grave;
that even if people praise us, because we are successful,
we will go under the ground
to meet our ancestors collected there in the darkness;
that we are all of us sheep, and death is our shepherd,
and we die as the animals die.

Ox Cart Man

In October of the year,
he counts potatoes dug from the brown field,
counting the seed, counting
the cellar's portion out,
and bags the rest on the cart's floor.

He packs wool sheared in April, honey
in combs, linen, leather
tanned from deerhide,
and vinegar in a barrel
hooped by hand at the forge's fire.

He walks by ox's head, ten days
to Portsmouth Market, and sells potatoes,
and the bag that carried potatoes,
flaxseed, birch brooms, maple sugar, goose
feathers, yarn.

When the cart is empty he sells the cart.
When the cart is sold he sells the ox,
harness and yoke, and walks
home, his pockets heavy
with the year's coin for salt and taxes,

and at home by fire's light in November cold
stitches new harness
for next year's ox in the barn,
and carves the yoke, and saws planks
building the cart again.

Old Roses

White roses, tiny and old, hover among thorns
by the barn door.
                For a hundred years
under the June elm, under the gaze
of seven generations,
                     they floated briefly,
like this, in the moment of roses,
                           by the fields
stout with corn, or with clover and timothy
making sweet hay,
                grown over, now,
with milkweed, sumac, paintbrush. . . .
                                Old
roses survive
winter drifts, the melt in April, August
parch,
    and men and women
who sniffed roses in spring and called them pretty
as we call them now,
                 strolling beside the barn
on a day that perishes. . . .

Names of Horses

All winter your brute shoulders strained against collars, padding
and steerhide over the ash hames, to haul
sledges of cordwood for drying through spring and summer,
for the Glenwood stove next winter, and for the simmering range.

In April you pulled cartloads of manure to spread on the fields,
dark manure of Holsteins, and knobs of your own clustered with
                                                                    oats.
All summer you mowed the grass in meadow and hayfield, the
                                                mowing machine
clacketing beside you, while the sun walked high in the morning;

and after noon's heat, you pulled a clawed rake through the same
                                                                    acres,
gathering stacks, and dragged the wagon from stack to stack,
and the built hayrack back, uphill to the chaffy barn,
three loads of hay a day from standing grass in the morning.

Sundays you trotted the two miles to church with the light load
of a leather quartertop buggy, and grazed in the sound of hymns.
Generation on generation, your neck rubbed the windowsill
of the stall, smoothing the wood as the sea smooths glass.

When you were old and lame, when your shoulders hurt bending
                                                            to graze,

one October the man, who fed you and kept you, and harnessed
you every morning,
led you through corn stubble to sandy ground above Eagle Pond,
and dug a hole beside you where you stood shuddering in your
skin,

and lay the shotgun's muzzle in the boneless hollow behind your
ear,
and fired the slug into your brain, and felled you into your grave,
shoveling sand to cover you, setting goldenrod upright above you,
where by next summer a dent in the ground made your monument.

For a hundred and fifty years, in the pasture of dead horses,
roots of pine trees pushed through the pale curves of your ribs,
yellow blossoms flourished above you in autumn, and in winter
frost heaved your bones in the ground—old toilers, soil makers:

O Roger, Mackerel, Riley, Ned, Nellie, Chester, Lady Ghost.

Stone Walls

1.

Stone walls emerge from leafy ground
and show their bones. In September a leaf
falls singly down, then a thousand leaves whirl
in frosty air. I am wild
with joy of leaves falling, of stone walls
emerging, of return to the countryside
where I lay as a boy
in the valley of noon heat, in the village
of little sounds; where I floated
out of myself, into the world that lives in the air.

In October the leaves turn
on low hills in middle distance, like heather, like tweed,
like tweed woven from heather and gorse,
purples, greens, reds, grays, oranges, weaving together
this joyful fabric,
and I walk in the afternoon sun, kicking the leaves.

In November the brightness washes from the hills
and I love the land most, leaves down, color drained out
in November rain,
everything gray and brown, against the dark evergreen,
everything rock and silver, lichen and moss on stone,
strong bones of stone walls showing at last
in November cold,
making wavy rectangles on the unperishing hills.

2.

Wesley Wells was my grandfather's name.
He had high cheekbones, and laughed as he hoed,
practicing his stories.

The first time I remember him, it was summer at twilight.
He was weak from flu, and couldn't hike for his cows
on Ragged Mountain; he carried the old chair with no back
that he used for milking
to the hillside over the house and called up-mountain:
"Ke-bosh, ke-bosh, ke-bo-o-o-o-sh, ke-bosh. . . ."

*   *   *

While he milked he told about drummers and base-ball,
he recited Lyceum poems about drunk deacons,
or about Lawyer Green, whose skin was the color green,
ridiculed as a schoolboy, who left town and returned triumphant . . .

and riding home from the hayfields, he handed me the past:
how he walked on a row of fenceposts
in the blizzard of eighty-eight; or sawed oblongs
of ice from Eagle Pond; or in summer
drove the hayrack into shallow water, swelling wooden
wheels tight inside iron rims;

or chatted and teased outside Amos Johnson's with Buffalo Billy
Fiske who dressed like a cowboy. . . .

While I daydreamed my schoolyear life
at Spring Glen Grammar School, or Hamden High,
I longed to return to him, in his awkward coat and cap,
in his sweater with many holes.

3.

A century ago these hills were bare;
you could see past Eagle Pond to sheep in the far pasture,
walls crossing cleared land, keeping Keneston
lambs from Peasly potatoes.

Today I walk in fields grown over—among
bare birches, oak saplings, enormous
sugar maples gone into themselves for winter—
beside granite that men stacked
"for twenty-five cents a rod, and forage
for oxen," boulders sledded into place,
smaller stones
fitted by clever hands to lock together, like the arched
ramparts at Mycenae.

I come to the foundations of an abandoned mill;
at the two sides of a trout stream, fieldstone walls emerging
uncut and unmortared
rear like a lion gate . . .
                              emptiness over
the still-rushing waters.

4.

Allende's murderers follow Orlando Letelier
to Washington; his car explodes when he turns the key.
His scream is distant, like the grocer's scream
stabbed in the holdup. . . . These howls—
and Tsvetayeva's in Yelabuga,
who hangs herself in her cottage—

                    pulse, reverberate, and die
in the scrub pine that grows from granite ledges
visible against snow at the top of Kearsarge,
because jamming plates drove
the Appalachian range through the earth crust
before men and women, before squirrels, before spruce and daisies,
when only amoebas wept
to divide from themselves. Stone dwindled
under millennial rain
like snowbanks in March, and diminished under glaciers,
under the eyes of mice and reindeer, under the eyes of foxes,
under Siberian eyes
tracking bear ten thousand years ago
on Kearsarge . . .

          and the Shah of Iran's opponents
wake to discover nails
driven through their kneecaps. When Pinochet frowns
in Chile, hearing these howls,
the corners of his mouth twitch with an uncontrollable grin;
Tiberius listening grins. . . .

Each morning we watch stone walls
emerge on Kearsarge and on Ragged Mountain;
I love these mountains which do not change.
The screams persist. I continue my life.

5.

At Thornley's Store,
the dead mingle with the living; Benjamin Keneston hovers
with Wesley among hardware; Kate looks over spools of thread
with Nanny, and old shadows stand among dowels and raisins,
woolen socks and axes. Now Ansel stops to buy salt
and tells Bob Thornley it got so cold he saw
two hounddogs put jumper cables on a jackrabbit.
Skiers stop for gas, summer people join us, hitchhikers,
roadworkers, machinists, farmers, saw-sharpeners;
our cries and hungers, stories and music reverberate
on the hills and stone walls, on the Exxon sign and clapboard
of Thornley's Store.

6.

At Church we eat squares of bread, we commune with mothers
and cousins, with mothering-fathering hills, with dead and living,
and go home in gray November, in Advent waiting,
among generations unborn
who will look at the same hills, as the leaves fall and turn gray,
and watch stone walls ascending Ragged Mountain.

*   *   *

These walls are the bones of Presidents, men and women
who were never born
and will never lead the Republic into the valley of cattle.

*   *   *

When gangs fight with dogs for the moose's body,
and poems for Letelier are scattered like the molecules of his body,
and the books are burnt, and this room wet ashes, and language
burnt out, and the dead departed along with the living,
wavering stone lines
will emerge from leaves in November, on mountains without
names.

*   *   *

Pole beans raise their green flags in the summer garden.
I grow old, in the house I wanted to grow old in.
When I am sleepy at night, I daydream only
of waking the next morning—to walk on the earth of the present
past noons of birch and sugarbush, past cellarholes,
many miles to the village of nightfall.

About the Author

DONALD HALL was a professor of English for nineteen years at the University of Michigan, and is the author of many books. Among his books of poetry are *The Yellow Room: Love Poems, A Roof of Tiger Lilies,* and *The Alligator Bride; Poems New and Selected.* His prose works include *Remembering Poets* (a memoir of Pound, Eliot, Frost and Dylan Thomas), *Henry Moore: the Life and Work of a Great Sculptor,* a collection of short stories, *String Too Short to Be Saved,* and a play about Robert Frost. He lives in Wilmot, New Hampshire, with his wife, the poet Jane Kenyon.